Discovering

SEA BIRDS

Anthony Wharton

Artwork by Wendy Meadway

The Bookwright Press
New York · 1987

Discovering Nature

Discovering Ants
Discovering Bees and Wasps
Discovering Beetles
Discovering Birds of Prey
Discovering Butterflies and Moths
Discovering Crabs and Lobsters
Discovering Crickets and Grasshoppers
Discovering Ducks, Geese and Swans
Discovering Flies
Discovering Flowering Plants

Discovering Frogs and Toads
Discovering Rabbits and Hares
Discovering Rats and Mice
Discovering Sea Birds
Discovering Slugs and Snails
Discovering Snakes and Lizards
Discovering Spiders
Discovering Squirrels
Discovering Worms

Further titles are in preparation

First published in the
United States in 1987 by
The Bookwright Press
387 Park Avenue South
New York, NY 10016

First published in 1987 by
Wayland (Publishers) Limited
61 Western Road, Hove
East Sussex BN3 1JD, England

ISBN: 0-531-18127-8
Library of Congress Catalog Card Number: 87–70038

Typeset by DP Press Limited, Sevenoaks, Kent
Printed in Italy by Sagdos S.p.A., Milan

Cover *Puffins on Skokholm Island, Wales.*

Frontispiece *The kittiwake is one of the smallest and most attractive gulls.*

Contents

1
Introducing Sea Birds

Gulls are probably the most common sea birds you will see on the coast. This is a herring gull.

What are Sea Birds?

People often think only of gulls when they hear the words "sea birds," but albatrosses, penguins, puffins and one kind of pelican are among the many other types. There are about 8,600 different kinds of birds in the world, of which only 285 are sea birds. Even so, sea birds are generally very numerous.

The most obvious reason why some birds are called sea birds is that they depend on the sea for their survival. They have all developed from land birds and have special features to help them overcome the harsh conditions found at sea.

Fish is the main food of many sea birds, and so the greatest numbers are found where the sea is rich in **plankton**. Many kinds of sea birds, however, stay within easy reach of land, and they are often said to be

"offshore" birds. Others prefer to roam the stormiest oceans. They are described as **pelagic**. The word "coastal" is used to describe those that spend most of their time on or over sea coasts. All sea birds have to come ashore to produce young.

Many sea birds, especially terns,

Unlike other kinds of pelicans, the brown pelican is a true sea bird.

migrate from one part of the world to another at different times of the year, often flying great distances. Others do not fly far at all, while a few, such as penguins, are completely flightless.

Sea Bird Groups of the World

There are four main groups of sea birds. Each group consists of a number of different families. A family is made up of several different but related birds.

Families such as gulls, terns, skuas, skimmers and auks all belong to one group. Apart from the auks, which include birds like puffins, guillemots and razorbills, the sea birds of this group are found in both **hemispheres**. The auks are found only in the northern hemisphere and are usually considered to be pelagic, although they find much of their food in shallow seas near the coasts. A few kinds of gulls and skimmers are found more on inland waters than at sea.

The second group contains all the

Common guillemots are members of the auk family.

different families of "tubenoses." These are birds whose nostrils open from horny tubes on their bills. They include albatrosses, shearwaters and petrels and they are all powerful fliers and are truly pelagic.

Cormorants, shags, gannets, boobies, frigate birds and pelicans make up the third group. They have four webbed toes instead of the more usual three, and many have a patch of bare skin on the throat. Most of the birds in this group are offshore birds.

The eighteen kinds of penguins belong to the fourth group and all live in the southern hemisphere. They cannot fly but they are excellent swimmers. They stand upright on land and have a comical walk, although they look very smart in their black and white **plumage**.

Gannets, like the other families in their group, have four webbed toes on each foot.

2
What Sea Birds Look Like

A cormorant drying its wings in the sun.

A Close Look at Sea Birds

There is no such creature as a "typical" sea bird. The many different kinds have developed in a variety of ways and differ widely in shape, size and color, as well as in their habits.

Despite such differences, sea birds have some common features. Their fairly short legs, with webbed feet, are usually set well back on their bodies. This means that many are clumsy when on land, although some kinds, such as gulls, can be quite nimble.

Another feature common to most sea birds is their dense plumage, which is kept waterproof with oil from a gland at the base of the tail. A layer of soft **down** beneath the surface helps prevent loss of body heat. A few kinds, such as cormorants are not truly waterproofed and can sometimes be seen spreading their wings to dry in the sun after they have

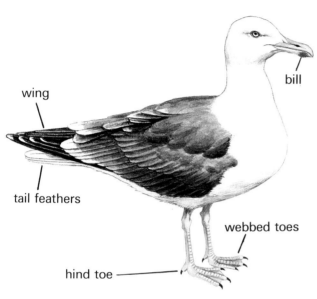

wing

bill

tail feathers

webbed toes

hind toe

All sea birds have webbed feet. These belong to a rockhopper penguin.

been in the water. Like other birds, sea birds replace their old feathers from time to time in a process called **molting**.

The wings of most sea birds have developed in one of two ways. Birds that spend a lot of their time in the air, such as albatrosses and terns, have long narrow wings for gliding and soaring. Wings of this type, however, are not very good for swimming underwater. Other kinds of sea birds have short, stubby wings, which are excellent for swimming but not so efficient in flight.

A royal albatross with its chick.

Shapes and Sizes

The bodies of many sea birds, such as albatrosses, penguins and pelicans, are quite stoutly built. Others, like those of terns and petrels, are fairly slender. All of them, however, are very **streamlined**.

Sea birds vary a lot in size, which helps us to identify the different kinds. The smallest sea bird, a least storm petrel, is only about 13 cm (5 in) in length. This is shorter than the bills of many albatrosses. The largest albatross has a wingspan of more than 360 cm (12 ft) and an emperor penguin may weigh as much as 40 kg (88 lb).

Sea birds' bills are very varied and can also help in identification. For example, most people can recognize a

The common tern is a slender, medium-sized bird with a daggerlike bill, long narrow wings and a forked tail.

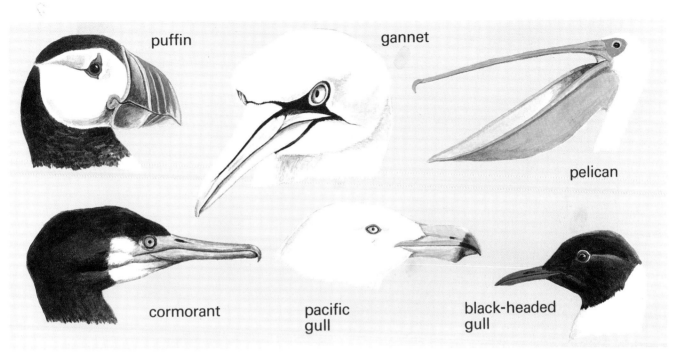

puffin

gannet

pelican

cormorant

pacific
gull

black-headed
gull

You can often identify a sea bird by its bill.

puffin because of its colorful, triangular bill. Pelicans, too, are easily recognized because of the shape of their pouched bills, which can hold up to 13.5 liters (3.5 gal) of water.

The bills of other sea birds may be daggerlike, like those of gannets, or long, slender and hooked at the tip, like those of cormorants and frigate birds. Gulls' bills vary a lot, from the stout bill of the Pacific gull, to the slender one of the European black-headed gull.

Sea birds' tails, too, can be of many different shapes. A gannet's tail is wedge-shaped, that of a tern or "sea-swallow" is forked, while a tropic bird's tail has streamers.

Colors and Plumage

Most sea birds do not have brightly colored plumage. Some, such as gulls and terns, are mainly white. A few, like cormorants and frigate birds, are mostly black or dark brown. The plumage of many kinds, however, is both black and white, or sometimes gray and white.

Males and females are usually very similar. Several kinds, such as emperor penguins and gannets, have yellow or orange in their plumage, particularly on the head or neck.

Most sea birds do not change color much when they molt, but a few show slight changes in color. The black-headed gull, for instance, has hardly any black on its head outside the **breeding season**.

The young of many sea birds take several years to develop their adult colors. Until this happens, they are often a mottled mixture of black, white and brown.

Although their plumage is not very colorful, many sea birds have

This is a puffin, easily recognized by its colorful triangular bill.

This nesting shag, a type of cormorant, has very black, glossy plumage.

A few sea birds, such as this king penguin, have yellow or orange on their heads.

brightly colored bills and feet. Pink, red and yellow are all very common. Puffins have perhaps the most colorful bills of all in the breeding season – a combination of all these colors, together with some blue.

Blue is often seen on the faces of some kinds of gannets, especially around the eyes. One kind of sea bird even has blue feet. The skin on the throats of certain of sea birds, especially those of the pelican family, is often brightly colored in the breeding season.

3
Sea Birds on the Move

A fulmar in flight is beautiful to watch.

In the Air

Many sea birds are excellent fliers. A fulmar, gliding along near the edge of a steep cliff, is a wonderful sight. The albatross, with its huge wingspan, can stay in the air for hours, perhaps days, almost without moving its wings, even in stormy weather. The flight of auks is very different. Guillemots and puffins fly quite fast with very rapid wingbeats.

Terns and gannets are beautiful in flight. They can hover well above the sea, before plunging into the water to catch fish. Petrels were perhaps named after St. Peter, because they appear to walk on water as they fly just above the surface of the sea looking for food. A flock of shearwaters, flying together can wheel and turn in formation.

Possibly the most efficient sea bird fliers are frigate birds or "man-o-war"

birds. Their flight looks very acrobatic as they change direction rapidly in pursuit of other birds.

It is not surprising that a group of birds that fly as well as sea birds should travel about the world as much as they do. However, strong winds sometimes blow them off course.

The gannet, with its long, narrow wings, is a strong flier. It can hover very easily in certain conditions.

Albatrosses, for example, are occasionally seen in the northern hemisphere, thousands of miles away from their normal **habitat**.

On and Under the Sea

Birds that depend on the oceans need to be excellent swimmers. Almost all sea birds can swim very well and many have folds of skin in their nostrils which they can close to prevent water from entering.

Gulls, as well as some other sea birds that are strong fliers, normally swim only on the surface. Others, which are less powerful in the air, seem as much at home beneath the surface as they are on top of it. Auks, for example, are very good under-water swimmers. They dive from the surface and use their short

Most gulls spend quite a lot of time on the surface of the water.

wings and their feet to propel themselves along. They look as if they are flying underwater. Puffins are also very agile beneath the surface of the water. They often catch ten or more fish during one dive.

Many other kinds of sea birds swim like auks, some using their tails as rudders. The Galapagos flightless cormorant, however, uses only its feet for swimming.

Penguins are probably the most efficient underwater swimmers and can reach speeds of 40 km (25 mi) an hour. Their poorly developed wings make excellent flippers. As they swim, only their backs and heads are visible, so they look somewhat like porpoises. They can jump straight out of the ocean at full speed onto a rock or an ice floe.

The poorly developed wings of penguins make excellent flippers.

The Miracle of Migration

Many kinds of sea birds do not stay in one area throughout the year. They fly away to spend the winter in a warmer place where there is more food. They often travel great distances. The Arctic tern, for example, flies 18,000 km (11,000 mi) from its breeding grounds in the northern hemisphere to spend the winter in the Antarctic. It flies back again in the spring.

Manx shearwaters are also long-distance travelers. They fly from their breeding **colonies** around the coasts of Britain and the Mediterranean to winter off the east coast of South America. A flight speed of more than 700 km (430 mi) a day means that they can reach Brazil in about 16 days.

Migrating sea birds probably use the sun and the stars to find their way. They do not often fly overland, but regularly follow coastlines. Many cross open seas and are therefore able to feed and rest easily.

The adults of some kinds of sea birds depart for their winter homes before their chicks can fly, leaving them to find their own way, even though they have never migrated before. Gannet chicks may even swim

The Manx shearwater, seen here at night outside its nest-burrow, is a long-distance traveler.

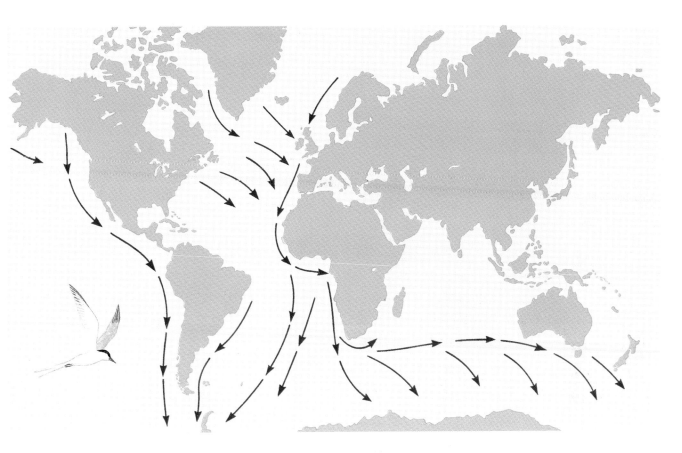

the first part of their journey.

Scientists have learned more about the migration of sea birds by putting small, numbered bands on their legs. Some birds are later caught or found dead elsewhere and the bands are

Arctic terns fly 18,000 km (11,000 mi) from their breeding grounds in the north to winter in the warmer Antarctic.

recovered to provide information about the birds' movements.

4
Food and Feeding

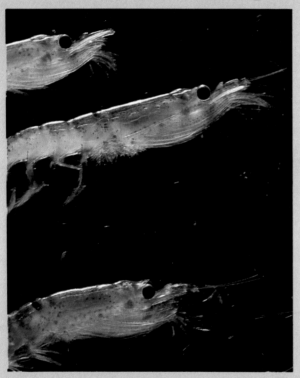

Small, shrimplike creatures called krill are very plentiful in Antarctic oceans. They are eaten by many sea birds.

Types of Food

Most sea birds eat fish, although many kinds eat other foods as well. The type and size of food depends a lot on the size of the bird and the way in which it feeds.

Albatrosses and penguins can swallow quite large fish, but the fish and other creatures eaten by small sea birds like storm petrels are very tiny. The auks, which are not very big, eat small fish such as sand eels and sprats.

Most other foods eaten by sea birds are also found in the sea or on the sea-shore. Shrimps, young crabs, squid, shellfish, jellyfish, marine worms, plankton and even baby turtles are all regularly eaten by sea birds. Flying fish form part of the diet of frigate birds and tropic birds.

Scavengers, such as gulls and skuas, will eat other sea birds, particularly their eggs and young.

A puffin eating sand eels.

Small mammals are not safe from them either. Many gulls are almost **omniverous**. In addition to the usual sea food, they will eat earthworms, vegetable matter and even people's garbage.

Young sea birds are fed by their parents until they are old enough to find their own food. Many, such as young tubenoses, eat an oily mixture brought up from their parents' stomachs. Others, like young terns or puffins, take freshly caught food directly from their parents' bills.

How Sea Birds Feed

Different sea birds have different ways of collecting food, although some use more than one method. Diving from the surface of the sea to chase **prey** underwater is one way. Cormorants, penguins, auks and diving petrels find most of their food by this method.

Albatrosses and some kinds of gulls are among the sea birds that find food while swimming or floating on the surface. Other kinds, such as storm

Black skimmers use the large lower mandible of their bills to scoop up food from the surface of the water.

Skuas and frigate birds often steal food from other birds. This is a long-tailed skua.

petrels, shearwaters and a few types of terns, gulls and skuas, dip into the water for food as they hover above it.

As its name suggests, the black skimmer picks up food by lowering the large lower **mandible** of its bill into the water as it skims along the surface. Gannets, boobies, brown pelicans and the larger terns like to fish by diving from the air into the sea, often from a height of many feet.

"Plunge-diving," as this method is called, is occasionally used by other kinds of sea birds.

Many kinds of gulls are scavengers and seem able to find food anywhere, even inland. Like albatrosses, fulmars and some other sea birds, they can sometimes be seen following ships to pick up food scraps that are thrown overboard.

Skuas and frigate birds often behave like pirates. They chase other sea birds to make them drop their prey, which they then steal.

5
Reproduction

Gannets nest just out of pecking range of each other.

Sea Bird Colonies

Most sea birds like to build their nests close to those of other birds of the same kind. Colonies, as these breeding groups are called, vary a lot in size. A colony may have fewer than 100 pairs of birds, or it may attract tens of thousands. Zavodoski Island, in the South Sandwich Islands, for example, has a huge colony of 10 million chinstrap penguins.

The distance between nests in a colony always seems to be roughly the same for a particular kind of sea bird. Gannets, for instance, build their nests about 80 cm (31 in) apart, so they are just out of pecking range of each other. Australian muttonbirds, on the other hand, nest closer together. There may be eight or nine of their nests in one square yard.

Sea bird colonies are mostly found on cliffs or small islands, from where

t is usually easy for the birds to
launch themselves into flight. In such
places they are also well protected
from most ground **predators**.
Protection from predators is probably
one of the main reasons why sea birds
nest so close together.

Gulls and terns often nest in mixed
colonies. Here Sandwich terns and
black-headed gulls nest side by side.

A few kinds of sea birds sometimes
form mixed colonies. Gulls and terns
do this regularly, as do razorbills and
guillemots.

Courtship and Display

When a sea bird is old enough to breed, it has to find both a **territory** and a mate. Which of these comes first depends on the type of sea bird. Male gannets and the males of some kinds of gulls, for example, choose their territories first, then look for mates. The males of many kinds of terns, on the other hand, choose their partners before looking for a home together.

In each case attracting a mate involves a sort of showing off, known as **courtship**, which is normally started by the male bird. Each kind of sea bird has its own way of showing off. A male frigate bird, for instance, develops a large red patch of bare skin on its throat during the breeding season. It shows off to its mate by puffing this up like a balloon. As it does so, it rattles its bill and cackles loudly. The many other types of courtship displays include "sky-pointing," "bill-clapping," "head-swaying," "see-sawing" and "wing-

These fulmars are fighting over the ownership of a territory.

A pair of Sandwich terns courting. The male has brought a fish as a gift.

drooping." Normally a female responds to a male's display with similar strange and comical antics until finally they become partners. The males often offer the females gifts of fish or seaweed. Sea birds that pair for life use displays to strengthen their partnerships.

Sea birds use displays to attract a mate.

bill-clapping

frigate bird puffing

see-sawing

gift of seaweed

sky-pointing

wing-drooping

Nests and Nest Sites

Each kind of sea bird has a favorite place to build its nest. Most kinds choose rocky ledges, cliff-top slopes, or the flatter parts of islands.

In many cases their nests are very simple affairs, while a few build no nest at all. Some kinds of albatrosses, for example, build very scanty nests and guillemots lay their single egg on a ledge of bare rock. On the other hand, the little kittiwake gull uses **guano** to stick its nest of seaweed and grass to a steep cliff face.

A herring gull at its nest among pebbles on a small island.

The kittiwake uses guano in the construction of its nest.

Puffins at their nest-burrows on top of a cliff.

Most gulls seem to be quite adaptable. They usually build fairly bulky nests out of vegetation and feathers, but sometimes include bits of paper or plastic, too. They may nest on cliff tops, on sand dunes or even on ledges of buildings.

Many kinds of terns choose sandy or pebbly seashores for nesting. Their nests are often only shallow scrapes in the ground. One kind of tern, however, the delicate fairy tern, lays its egg on the bare branch of a tree. Other tree-nesting sea birds include the brown pelican and the red-footed booby, a type of gannet.

Some birds make their nests in holes. Puffins, for instance, dig their own burrows or take over rabbit holes on the tops of cliffs. Many kinds of shearwaters and petrels, as well as the fairy penguin, also nest in burrows.

Eggs and Young

Sea birds' eggs vary in size, color, and in the number laid. Usually the size of the egg varies according to the size of the bird that lays it. For their size and weight, however, penguins, pelicans, gannets and cormorants lay surprisingly small eggs. On the other hand, some tubenoses lay quite large eggs for their size.

This clutch of three eggs belongs to a pair of lesser black-backed gulls.

The eggs of gulls, terns and auks are colored in shades of green or beige, with some darker blotches on them. This means that they are quite well **camouflaged**, especially those of the ground-nesting terns. Sea birds such as albatrosses, penguins and fulmars, have plain, light-colored eggs, even though they nest in the open. Burrow-nesters usually lay white eggs.

Some sea birds, such as gannets, lay only one egg, although many kinds lay two. **Clutches** of three or four are found mainly among terns and gulls. Sea bird eggs do not vary much in shape, although those that are laid on bare rock ledges are often pear-shaped so that they roll around in small circles, instead of falling off.

The eggs of most sea birds are **incubated** by both parents. It takes almost 80 days for some albatross eggs to hatch, and an incubation period of between 35 and 60 days is

Sea bird chicks, like these young gulls, are born with a covering of down to keep them warm.

quite common among other sea birds.

Most sea bird chicks are born with a covering of thick down, which is very soft and warm. They usually stay in the nest for quite a long time. Young albatrosses stay for more than thirty weeks, although herring gull chicks may leave after only a day or two.

6
Sea Birds and People

Razorbills are among the first sea birds to suffer when there is an oil spill. This young razorbill cannot walk or fly.

People as a Threat

Since ancient times people have considered sea birds good to eat. Countless numbers have been killed for food, particularly on North Atlantic coasts and on islands in the southern hemisphere. So many birds have been killed, especially ground-nesting kinds, that some are now **extinct**. The flightless great auk, for instance, disappeared from the North Atlantic in about 1844. It was not afraid of people and was easily clubbed to death. Gannets, puffins and short-tailed shearwaters from Australia are among the sea birds that have been killed by the thousands.

The eggs of sea birds have also been collected for food in huge numbers. Even today, sea birds and their eggs are taken for food in some parts of the world. Disturbance by people and by animals that people have introduced

to sea bird islands, has also done great damage.

In recent times many sea birds have been killed by oil that leaks or is discharged into the sea from tankers. Oil spills may have killed as many as 500,000 birds in a single incident. Few birds can survive, once they are covered with oil, as they can neither

This is a museum specimen of the great auk, which became extinct in about 1844.

fly nor swim.

Some sea birds, especially gulls, can be a threat to people. They can spread disease by polluting water supplies. They also sometimes crash into aircraft in flight and cause accidents.

New Opportunities

Certain kinds of sea birds have taken advantage of the activities of people. The fishing and whaling industries, for example, may have been the main cause of increases in the numbers of certain sea birds. Fulmars now breed widely around much of Britain's coastline, although there were very few of them 100 years ago. This is perhaps due to the large quantities of **offal** thrown overboard from trawlers and whaling ships. Fulmars are among those sea birds that eat this kind of food.

Herring gulls have also increased in numbers. They have learned to scavenge around places where people live and work. They can often be seen looking for food on docks and on rubbish heaps. You may have seen flocks of gulls following tractors as they plow fields. They have learned that there is often food to be found in newly plowed fields. In some places herring gulls, fulmars and kittiwakes have started to use buildings as nesting sites, instead of their usual nesting places on sea cliffs.

Herring gulls and black-backed gulls often increase in numbers in places where people give protection to colonies of birds such as terns. If their

Fulmars, members of the order of tubenoses, have increased greatly in numbers in the last 100 years.

numbers increase too much, so that they become a danger to other birds, they have to be **culled**.

Lesser black-backed gulls sometimes become too numerous because of the protection given to sea birds such as terns.

Protection

It should be clear from what you have already read that sea birds need protection from people. Long ago the Incas of Peru realized this and protected sea bird colonies near their coast.

Only recently, however, have

The tiny island of Grassholm is a reserve where thousands of pairs of gannets nest.

people become truly concerned about the welfare of birds. In this century many countries have passed laws to protect birds. As a result, some populations of sea birds that were in danger are now growing again.

The International Council for Bird Protection has branches in many countries. One of its main concerns is the growing threat to sea birds of oil **pollution**, which it tries hard to prevent.

Sea birds can also be protected by the setting up of special **reserves**, where they can breed without disturbance. In Alaska, for example, the Pribilof Islands are part of the Alaska Maritime Wildlife Refuge. Over 2.8 million sea birds nest there. Far away in the Leeward Islands of Hawaii, the National Wildlife Refuge protects the rookeries of petrels, shearwaters, boobies, terns, frigate birds and albatrosses.

Little terns are strictly protected in Britain.

Volunteer organizations play a vital part, too. For example, a Bird Rescue and Research Clinic in Pennsylvania has conducted important studies on the effect of oil spills. The clinic is run by volunteers. As individuals, we too can help by joining bird protection societies.

7
Studying Sea Birds

The things you will need for watching sea birds are binoculars, a field guide for identifying the birds you see, a notebook and a pencil.

We can all learn a lot about sea birds from books. However, it is much more exciting to study them by actually watching them.

Unfortunately, many sea birds are difficult to watch outside the breeding season, as they spend so much time at sea. Even during the breeding season, many kinds are found only on dangerous cliffs, while others, such as shearwaters and petrels, are seen on land only at night. Nevertheless it is well worth the effort if you can visit colonies of sea birds such as gulls, terns and gannets.

To watch sea birds you will need some basic equipment, such as a field guide, some binoculars and a notebook. A field guide is a book with pictures and descriptions of the birds you are likely to see. Binoculars make distant birds seem closer and clearer. The most suitable ones have the numbers 8×40 or 7×50 marked on